GREAT EXPLORATIONS

VASCO DA GAMA

So Strong a Spirit

Patricia Calvert

BENCHMARK BOOKS

MARSHALL CAVENDISH
NEW YORK

With special thanks to Serinity Young, Ph.D., American Museum of Natural History, for her careful reading of this manuscript.

For Paul and Sheila Wellstone,
in memoriam

Benchmark Books
99 White Plains Road
Tarrytown, NY 10591-9001
www.marshallcavendish.us

Library of Congress Cataloging-in-Publication Data

Calvert, Patricia.
Vasco da Gama : so strong a spirit / Patricia Calvert.
p. cm. — (Great explorations)
Includes timeline.
Summary: Recounts the voyages undertaken by fifteenth-century Portuguese explorer Vasco da Gama to strengthen his nation's power by establishing a sea trade route to India.
Includes bibliographical references and index.
ISBN 0-7614-1611-0
1. Gama, Vasco da, 1469–1524—Juvenile literature. 2. Explorers—Portugal—Biography—Juvenile literature. 3. Discoveries in geography—Portuguese—Juvenile literature. [1. Gama, Vasco da, 1469–1524. 2. Explorers. 3. Discoveries in geography.] I. Title. II. Series.

G286.G2C28 2004
910'.92—dc22

2003022946

Photo research by Candlepants Incorporated

Cover photo: Service Historique de la Marine, Vincennes, France/Lauros/Giraudon/Bridgeman Art Library
Cover inset: Private Collection/Bridgeman Art Library

The photographs in this book are used by permission and through the courtesy of: *Corbis*: Tony Arruza, 5; Archivo Iconographico S.A., 17; Bettmann, 47. *North Wind Picture Archive*: 7, 55, 65, 68. *Art Resource*: Scala, 9; Erich Lessing, 23; The Pierport Morgan Library, 25, 76; Victoria & Albert Museum, London, 48, 58; Nicolas Sapieha, 53; Giradon, 84. *The Art Archive*: Marine Museum Lisbon/Dagli Orti,11; Science Academy, Lisbon/Dagli Orti ,27; Museo Historico Nacional Rio de Janeiro Brazil/Dagli Orti, 63; Arquivo Nacional da Torre do Tombo Lisbon/Dagli Orti, 71; Museo de Arte Antiga Lisbon/Dagli Orti, 74. *The Bridgeman Art Library*: Private Collection/The Stapleton Collection, 14; University of Witwatersrand, Johannesburg, South Africa, 20-21; Science Academy Lisbon/Dagli Orti, 27; Private Collection, 29; Royal Geographical Society, London, UK, 32; British Library, London, UK, 35; The Stapleton Collection, 43; Banco Nacional Ultramarino, Portugal, 45; Banco Nacional Ultramarino, Portugal, 50; Private Collection, 60; Musee Conde, Chantilly, France, 72; National Museum of Ancient Art, Lisbon, Portugal, 79; Lisbon, Portugal, 82.

Printed in China
3 5 6 4 2

Contents

foreword

Raw courage led Portuguese explorers such as Vasco da Gama and his countryman, Ferdinand Magellan, to seek new lands during Portugal's Age of Discovery, which lasted from about 1415 to 1520. Courage alone would not have been enough, however, without the improvements in shipbuilding during the fifteenth century that made long ocean voyages possible.

Until then, European ships had been of two main designs: one from the North and one from the Mediterranean. One way the two types of vessels differed was in the shape and number of their sails. In northern Europe, ships used a "square-rigged" design, a single square sail attached to a main mast. In southern Europe, "lateen-rigged" ships had two or three masts and triangular sails. Square-riggers moved well when the wind came from behind them, but they were hard to handle when the wind blew from the side. The opposite was true for lateen-riggers.

The designs of the ships' hulls, or outer frames, were different too. The planks of northern ships overlapped like shingles on a roof. The planks of southern, or Mediterranean, ships—called caravels—were snugly fitted edge to edge. As a result, caravels cut more swiftly through the water. The genius of Portuguese shipbuilders was to combine the best elements of both northern and southern designs.

"More than any other European nation, Portugal launched the Age of Discovery," wrote Angus Konstam, curator of arms and armor at the Tower of London. Yet tiny Portugal, lying on the western edge of Europe, was in many ways an unlikely candidate for such high honor.

The country is shaped like a narrow box—362 miles (583 km) from north to south and about 140 miles (225 km) wide from east to west—

Portuguese shipbuilders combined the best elements of northern and southern European ship design to create a faster, more reliable vessel.

comparable to the state of Indiana in square miles. In the second century B.C.E., the Romans named the country's best harbor *Portus Cale*, or "warm port," from which the nation's name was derived.

With few natural resources, no standing army, and less than a million people, there was only one way Portugal could compete in world affairs: by going to sea. Encouraged by their shipbuilding skills and superior designs, Portuguese seamen took to the open seas. It was often said that they "did not fear their fate too much."

Nor did the three oldest sons of King John I of Portugal fear their fates. When their father planned a fancy coming-of-age celebration for them, the princes—Duarte, Pedro, and Henry—suggested something bolder. They proposed an attack on the Muslim seaport of Ceuta, south of the Strait of Gibraltar in present-day Morocco. Ceuta was the endpoint of many caravan routes from the east, including one that transported gold from the interior of Africa.

Prince Henry (1394–1460), the king's third son, was a student of history and geography. He pointed out that the capture of Ceuta—called "the key to the Mediterranean" because it was where Muslim invaders entered Spain in 711 C.E.—would not only give Portugal access to the riches that poured into Muslim hands. Its countryside boasted large herds of cattle and sheep, as well as fields of wheat, which was often hard to grow in stony Portugal. Just as importantly, Henry believed the *Moors*—the term Europeans used for Muslims in Africa—could be Christianized.

King John I approved his sons' plan, as did the Portuguese Royal Council. On July 25, 1415, the feast day of St. James, twenty-one-year-old Henry and his older brothers set forth to besiege Ceuta. Three weeks later, on August 15, they came ashore and defeated the Moors on the city streets.

After such an easy victory, Prince Henry decided that Portugal could "do by sea [what] for many years [others] had done by land"—that is, it could find a sea road to the richest kingdom of all, India. He established a school in the Algarve, Portugal's southernmost province, to teach Portuguese

The successful siege of Cueta in 1415 first proved to the small nation of Portugal that it could be a dominant force on the world stage.

seamen the latest techniques of navigation, astronomy, and mapmaking. He was so successful that he came to be called Prince Henry the Navigator.

By 1419 Portuguese seamen began exploring the coast of Africa. Fifteen expeditions tried but failed to round Cape Bojador on the upper western edge of the continent. But by 1434 Gil Eannes had accomplished that feat. Then in 1436 Afonso Baldaya traveled 500 miles (800 km) farther. Nuno Tristado discovered the mouth of Africa's Senegal River in 1444. Pedro da Sintra sighted the mountains of Sierra Leone in 1460. Prince Henry died that year, never to witness his dream come true. But Portugal's sailors continued in their pursuit of Asian markets.

In 1488 Bartolomeu Dias finally rounded the tip of southern Africa. Before him lay the vast Indian Ocean. Now all Portugal needed was the right man to realize Prince Henry's ambitions and to extend that country's dominance and influence to the coast of India.

ONE

To You Alone
I Give Command

Prince Henry died on November 13, 1460, at age sixty-six. He never married; he left no son to continue the mission to which he'd devoted his life.

The year that Henry died, Estavan da Gama celebrated the birth of his third son, Vasco, in the village of Sines. Historians cannot document the precise month and day. A small seaport facing the Atlantic, Sines lay halfway between Lisbon and Cape St. Vincent. A ten-minute walk from the village brought one to a snug harbor shielded by a 60-foot-high (18-m) granite wall, where ships rested safely no matter how fierce the weather.

The da Gamas were descended from a nobleman who had battled against Moorish invaders in 1166. In 1250 another ancestor, Alvaro Annes da Gama, fought bravely against the Moors in the Algarve. The family was not rich, nor could it boast any royal blood in its veins. Nevertheless the family was respected for its "long and honorable history."

Prince Henry of Portugal (1394–1460) established a school of
navigation to train his nation's seamen. He is known today
as Henry the Navigator and was the author of Portugal's plan
to dominate the markets of the East.

9

Estavan da Gama was the *alcaide-mór*, or mayor, of Sines, which meant he commanded the white-walled fortress located on the cliff above the sea. His position allowed Estavan to provide the best education for his son Vasco as well as for the boy's older brothers, Paulo and Ayres. By the time Vasco was seven, Prince Henry had become one of his heroes.

Details of Vasco's early boyhood are sketchy. Even though he was a *fidalgo*—the son of a nobleman—he no doubt spent countless hours with the children of the local sailors and fishermen. From them he

THE INFAMY OF THE INQUISITION

In medieval times, the population of Spain was almost equally divided among three religious groups—Catholics, Muslims, and Jews. In 1478 with the hearty approval of her consort, King Ferdinand, Queen Isabella sought to unify her religious, political, and economic power by suppressing any hint of heresy—that is, any belief in a faith other than the Roman Catholic Church. Many Muslims and Jews had no alternative but to convert, if in name only, to avoid harassment or death. This desire to stamp out heresy quickly spread throughout the Iberian Peninsula. The Portuguese were also caught up in the hysteria targeting Muslims, Jews, or any believers of another faith, and thousands were put to death at Évora.

learned how to swim, fish, and handle the small sailboats in the harbor. He also learned to navigate by the stars, read the ocean's currents, and interpret the mood of the clouds overhead. Vasco probably listened intently to tales told by his friends' fathers—stories about storms at sea, of landings on foreign shores, and of exotic plants and animals in countries with strange names.

When it was time to attend school, Vasco was sent to Évora, a larger village about 70 miles (113 km) northeast of Sines. It had been founded by the ancient Celts and later occupied by the Romans. Its narrow streets had colorful names, such as Lane of the Cats, Alley of the Little Devil, and Road of the Ax. There was a black chapter in Évora's history, too. It was there in 1478 that an estimated 22,000 victims of the Inquisition were burned at the stake.

At Évora, da Gama learned the type of advanced mathematics and principles of navigation that prepared him for life at sea. By age fifteen, he had been aboard trading ships that had docked at ports along the west coast of Africa. He was remembered by some as "bold [and] daring." Others

Vasco da Gama (1460–1524) grew up among the sons of fishermen and sailors in the coastal town of Sines. The sea became a second home to him, and he later went on to fulfill the dreams of Prince Henry the Navigator.

noted that he was also "quick to anger, even more so than his brothers." Among their peers, the da Gama men had a reputation "not only for bravery, but also for being very quarrelsome." Vasco, a short, burly, black-bearded fellow with a hooked nose and slanted eyes, had an intense, hawkish appearance that matched his nature. By the time he was twenty, he was the captain of a ship. Most importantly, he'd become a respected member of the court of King John II, called "John the Perfect" by his subjects.

In keeping with Prince Henry's ambitions, Portuguese sailors continued to brave the west coast of Africa in search of the elusive sea route to India. Da Gama was twenty-eight years old when one of King Henry's sailors, Bartolomeu Dias, rounded the Cape of Good Hope in 1488. Ambitious navigators such as da Gama waited impatiently for the next phase of exploration to begin.

Repeating Dias's accomplishment was difficult. King John II feared that his small country would become involved in conflicts with more powerful nations—in particular, its hostile neighbor, Spain—if Portugal tried to expand its trade routes. Then, in 1495, seven years after Dias's discovery, John the Perfect died.

The king's twenty-four-year-old cousin, Manuel I, came to the throne in October of that year. Manuel I was not as timid as John and pushed Portugal to expand its trade routes. Bartolomeu Dias probably expected to be named the *capitao-mór*, or captain-major, of the fleet and certainly deserved the honor, but surprisingly, King Manuel's choice was thirty-seven-year-old Vasco da Gama. Gaspar Correa, an eyewitness to the events, described how King Manuel made his decision. "One day the king, sitting in his hall of business at a table with his officers, giving orders, by chance . . . raised his eyes, and Vasco da Gama happened to cross through the hall. . . . The king, setting eyes upon him . . . was transported [entranced]."

A MAN TO WATCH

Vasco da Gama's reputation as a man who knew a great deal about "affairs of the sea" gained increasing notice at court. Not only was da Gama an experienced navigator, he was a great leader and diplomat. In 1492 when the French captured a Portuguese caravel loaded with gold (even though Portugal and France were supposedly at peace), King John II ordered the capture of ten French vessels lying in Lisbon's harbor. Their sails and tillers (steering devices) were removed to prevent their escape. Then he sent for da Gama. "Do any and all things necessary" to resolve the matter with the French, he ordered. The outcome was what King John II desired—the French king apologized, and the Portuguese caravel was returned "in the manner in which it had been taken . . . without a doubloon [gold coin] missing."

What was there in Vasco's manner that "transported" the young king? It wasn't the first time he had seen da Gama, who often appeared at court. Was it something in his swagger, the fact that he was known to be a shrewd commander of men? Whatever it was, Manuel I hung his hopes for Portugal's future on a gut reaction that told him da Gama was his man.

King Manuel told da Gama, "My heart tells me that my desire will be accomplished by you . . . [and] to you alone, I give the command."

Then Manuel asked if da Gama had any brothers who could command one of the other ships, urging him to select someone "according to your will and pleasure." Vasco declared that he did indeed have a brother, more than one in fact. It was his oldest brother, Paulo, that he had in mind. "Call him to go with you," suggested the king. But Paulo—as hot tempered as the other men in the da Gama line—had attacked and wounded a judge in a quarrel in the nearby town of Setúbal. He'd gone into hiding, was a fugitive from justice, and would be arrested the moment he reappeared. "For love of you, I pardon him," Manuel promised. "Let him come at once and not delay."

Paulo gladly accepted the king's pardon and the chance to join his brother in such an adventure. Nicolas Coelho, whom da Gama had

---

*After Vasco da Gama's discovery of a sea route to India,
the Portuguese port capital of Lisbon became
one of the richest cities in Europe.*

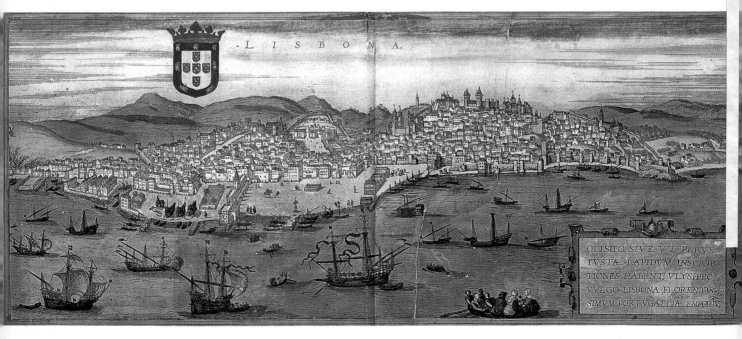

known since boyhood, was given command of a third ship. When the sailors were recruited for the journey, Vasco warned that they would need to do more than hoist (lift) or lower sails, as the voyage would be a long one. He gave each man an extra stipend, or payment, and told him to learn as much about carpentry, rope making, caulking, plank making, and blacksmithing as possible before the fleet departed.

FREEDOM AND AN UNCERTAIN FATE

Da Gama requested that convicts be included in his crew. Ten such men, condemned to death by hanging, were promised their freedom when and if they returned alive. No doubt the prisoners were glad to be spared, but they had no idea how da Gama planned to use them. Da Gama intended "to adventure them," that is, to put them ashore to gather information, locate villages, and act as messengers in places where the greatest danger was expected. He also planned to leave some of them permanently behind in foreign lands, "where, if they survived, they might prove of value . . . when he returned and found them again." When da Gama left one of the criminals, John Machado, in Mozambique, a fellow prisoner, Damiao Rodrigues, leaped off the ship in the dark and swam to join his friend. Rodrigues died, but Machado made his way to India, where he became a respected official.

Bartolomeu Dias accompanied the voyage in his own vessel as far as the Cape Verde Islands. It was a mark of Dias's character that he gave da Gama advice, helping him to design the kind of ships—ones with wide, round hulls that "rode the water like ducks"—to better withstand the stormy seas that they would face on the journey around the cape.

Da Gama realized that they needed interpreters on their voyage, so he recruited three men. Martin Affonso had lived in the Congo and knew many African dialects. Fernando Martins spoke Arabic, while John Nunes spoke both Arabic and Hebrew.

Before his departure, da Gama was summoned to court and was presented with the banner of the Knights of Christ, a white silk flag with a large red cross emblazoned in its center. Da Gama swore to King Manuel "on the symbol of this cross . . . [that] I shall uphold it and not surrender it in sight of the Moor." The mission to drive the Muslims out of Africa was second only to finding a route to India.

Da Gama's flagship was the 120-ton (108-metric-ton) *São Gabriel* (*são* means "saint"). The *São Raphael*, commanded by Paulo da Gama, weighed the same, while Nicolas Coelho's ship, the *Berrio*, was the lightest at 50 tons (45 metric tons). The largest vessel, the 200-ton (181-metric-ton) *São Maria* commanded by Gonçalvo Nunes, was a storeship loaded with enough food and supplies to last three years. It also carried *padrões*, or carved stone columns to be planted along the coast to mark the explorer's passage and to claim the route in Portugal's name. For protection, the vessels were armed with bombards, or catapults that hurled stone balls, to fend off possible attacks.

The night before the fleet left Portugal, Vasco, Paulo, and the other two captains attended an all-night vigil in the *ermida*, or small chapel, of Our Lady of Bethlehem in Restello, built years before by

ANCIENT ENEMIES

With the collapse of the Roman Empire in the fifth century C.E., the Christian West fell into chaos. In the East, however, a powerful new religion, Islam, emerged in the early seventh century under the leadership of the Arab prophet, Mohammed. Its followers called themselves Muslims, which means, "those who have surrendered themselves." Within one hundred years, all of Arabia and parts of North Africa, the Middle East, and Asia Minor had converted to the new faith. Just as importantly, the rich trade routes that coursed through some of these regions also fell under Muslim control. In the West, the Moors invaded Spain and Portugal and were about to enter France when they were driven back. In 1096 Europeans launched the first of eight Crusades, or holy wars, as East and West struggled to impose their beliefs on each other and to control access to the wealth of the East.

The Moors—followers of the Muslim faith—controlled the rich trade routes of the East for centuries. In 1096 Europeans launched the first of several Crusades, or holy wars, against them.

Prince Henry. At dawn on Saturday, July 8, 1497, da Gama led his four ships out of the harbor. When the wind filled their sails, it could be seen that a large red cross had been painted on each piece of canvas. Many on shore wept, knowing they might never see their husbands, sons, or brothers again. Were the sailors glad to go? Regardless, the adventure they were embarking on would make King Manuel I—remembered as "the Fortunate"—the richest monarch in all of Europe.

TWO

An Act of
Audacity

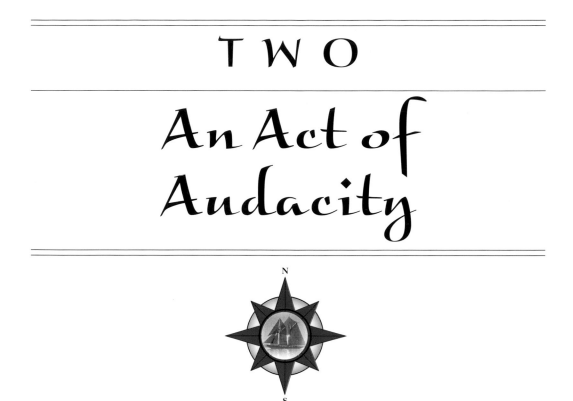

On Saturday, July 15, 1497, a week after leaving Lisbon, da Gama's fleet sighted the Canary Islands. The weather was mild, and the waters along the coast were so calm that members of the crew dropped fishing lines overboard and caught fish for supper. Two days later, however, thick fog rolled in during the night, and, in the morning, the *São Gabriel* found itself alone on a deserted sea.

Da Gama was well acquainted with the ocean's unpredictability and had issued orders for regrouping if the fleet became separated. "We therefore made sail for the Cape Verde islands as we had been instructed to do," wrote the author of the ship's logbook. On July 22, the other vessels were sighted, and five days later the entire fleet dropped anchor in the harbor at Santiago, the largest of the Cape Verde Islands. There the crew was allowed shore leave; sails were checked and mended; fresh meat, water, and wood were taken aboard.

On August 3 the fleet left Santiago. Rather than stick close to the African coast, knowing that the remaining distance to the Cape of Good Hope was enormous—4,500 miles (7,250 km)—da Gama charted a bold course. He headed southwest, far out into the Atlantic in order to take advantage of the fair winds and favorable ocean currents. His decision, called an "act of superlative audacity," would have seemed even more daring if anyone had realized the fleet almost reached the coast of Brazil, a land whose existence was unknown in Europe at that time.

Later the fleet's course was reset, and it headed south and east. Weeks drifted by with no land sighted. The daily monotony was broken only by storms. August and September passed. Fresh fruits and vegetables, high in vitamin C, ran out. Soon men began to suffer from scurvy, a terrible disease. Beriberi, a disease caused by the lack of vitamin B1,

In a symbolic act, King Manuel I had presented Vasco da Gama with the banner of the Knights of Christ. It reminded the explorer of the importance of his mission. The hopes of an entire nation rested on him and his crew.

or thiamine, also became a problem. Water supplies ran low, and sailors were limited to a *quarthilo*, or one-and-a-half cups, per day.

On Friday, October 27, 1497, *golfao*, a type of seaweed common along the southwestern coast of Africa, appeared on the ocean's surface. Birds circled overhead. Whales and *lobo marinho*, or sea wolves, a name given to many kinds of seals, were spotted. This all meant that land was near, and on Wednesday, November 1—All Saints' Day on the Christian calendar—the fleet entered a broad, sheltered bay that da Gama named St. Helena.

Soundings, or measurements, to estimate the water's depth were taken to be sure it was safe to drop anchor, and seven days later, men were sent ashore to search for water and food. The sailors spied two native residents gathering honey from sandy mounds along the beach.

THE ROTEIRO

The identity of the author of the *Roteiro*, the logbook that was kept of da Gama's first voyage around the Cape of Good Hope, isn't known. Some historians believe it was written by da Gama himself. However, "No one has yet succeeded in discovering the author of the *Roteiro*," British historian E. G. Ravenstein admitted in 1898. The writer was most likely a common sailor or soldier, because he frequently referred to *nos outros*, or "we others," as if to distinguish between officers and ordinary crew members such as himself. Also the style of the narrative points to its author's "humble condition." The *Roteiro* was published for the first time in Portugal in 1838. A French translation followed in 1855 and an English version in 1869. Regardless of the author's true identity, the *Roteiro* has become a trusted resource for historians.

Using smoking torches to drive the bees away from their hives, they were so intent on their task they didn't notice the strangers who had come ashore.

When the sighting of the native peoples was reported to da Gama, he ordered that they be captured. One escaped, but the other was taken aboard da Gama's ship. He trembled in fear and "seemed to sob" but was fed, given clothing as well as small bells and beads, then released

Portuguese ships, pictured in this detail from a seventeenth-century carpet, were built with wide, round hulls to better navigate the often rough waters of the South Atlantic.

unharmed. The next morning, fifteen native residents appeared on shore—"tawny-coloured [and] dressed in skins . . . accompanied by many dogs that resembled those of Portugal." They accepted small gifts, and on November 12, about fifty more appeared. They were given *ceitils*, or copper coins.

One of da Gama's men-at-arms, Fernand Veloso, asked permission to accompany these locals back to see what they ate and how they lived. Da Gama refused, but Paulo urged him to reconsider. Hours after da

THE HORRORS OF SCURVY

Scurvy, a disease caused by the lack of vitamin C, was well known to seafarers from the earliest of times. It was said that the suffering of the men in da Gama's fleet would have been far worse had it not been for "the kindliness of Paulo da Gama . . . [who] visited the sick both night and day, and . . . ministered to them," sharing remedies he had brought for his own use. Jean Mocquet, who traveled to Africa a century later, described his own ordeal: "[Scurvy] rotted my gums," he wrote, "which gave out a black and putrid blood. . . . My thighs and lower legs were black and gangrenous [decaying] . . . each day . . . I had to cut away this dead flesh. . . . Many of our people died . . . their eyes and the soles of their feet gnawed away by rats. . . . Among us was the greatest confusion and chaos imaginable, because of the great number of men . . . vomiting . . . [who] appeared bereft of reason."

Gama had agreed, shouts were heard from the beach. Veloso could be seen trying to outrun angry native peoples armed with bows, arrows, and stones. Da Gama himself rowed a skiff ashore to assist the others in Veloso's rescue and was lightly wounded in the leg by an arrow.

What Veloso did to anger the locals wasn't recorded in the *Roteiro*, but it was noted that the incident "happened because we looked upon

As Vasco da Gama's fame and respect grew over the course of his life,
he dressed and acted the part. To some, the explorer eventually
took on the aspect of a king.

these people as men of little spirit, quite incapable of violence, and had therefore landed without first arming ourselves." It was a mistake da Gama wouldn't repeat, but the encounter meant that the harbor was no longer safe. The fleet left on November 14.

Da Gama knew he must be close to the Cape of Good Hope. He was right. On November 18, "we beheld the Cape." The winds were unfavorable, however, and the cape couldn't be doubled, or gone around. Finally, on Wednesday, November 22, the fleet doubled the cape, more than five months after departing from Lisbon. On St. Catherine's Day, November 25, the four Portuguese ships entered Mossel Bay and remained there for thirteen days, where "we broke up our store-ship and transferred her contents to the other vessels." In 1488 Dias had landed at Mossel Bay himself, leaving behind an unfortunate legacy—he had killed one of the native residents with an arrow from a crossbow.

A week later, the explorers were greeted by 200 people driving oxen, cows, and sheep before them, some carrying *goras*, or native flutes, on which they piped a tune of welcome. Dias's act of murder had apparently been forgiven. With Martin Affonso acting as a translator, the meat-starved Portuguese traded three inexpensive bracelets for a black ox.

"We found him very fat, and . . . as toothsome as the beef of Portugal," noted the author of the *Roteiro*. The encounter seemed peaceful, so da Gama planted a stone *padrão* on the beach, with a large wooden cross made from a spare ship's mast. "When about to set sail," however, "we saw about ten or twelve negroes . . . [demolish] the cross and the pillar." The death nine years earlier hadn't been forgotten after all.

By Christmas Day 1497, the fleet had proceeded "seventy leagues" (a league is approximately 3 miles or 4.8 km), or more than 200 miles (322 km) beyond the last *padrão* Dias had planted. The coast they had been sailing along was beautiful, and da Gama named it Natal, in honor of Jesus's birth. By January 11, 1498, the fleet had anchored near a coun-

·S· [] grarriel

𝕮 Vasquo da gama, 𝕯

The wooden planks used in making the Portuguese caravel
were fitted snugly edge to edge, which enabled the ship
to move smoothly across the water.

try of "tall people" and stayed five days. Interpreter Martin Affonso and another sailor were sent ashore, where locals offered them a porridge (a stew) of millet and cooked fowl, "just like those of Portugal." In return, the chief was given a jacket, red trousers, a cap, and a bracelet.

Three months later, on Friday, March 2, 1498, da Gama encountered a much different population at Mozambique, a low-lying port midway up the east coast of Africa. Mozambique wasn't a simple settlement, as

TERRA DA BOA GENTE, LAND OF GOOD PEOPLE

"The houses [here] are built of straw," noted the author of the *Roteiro*. "The arms [weapons] of the people include long bows and arrows and spears with iron blades. Copper seems to be plentiful, for the people wore [ornaments] of it on their legs and arms and in their twisted hair. Tin, likewise, is found in the country, for it is to be seen on the hilts of their daggers, the sheaths of which are made of ivory. Linen cloth is highly prized by the people, who were always willing to give large quantities of copper in exchange for shirts. They have large calabashes [gourds] in which they carry sea-water inland [then] pour it into pits, to obtain salt [by evaporation]. . . . We called the country *Terra da Boa Gente* [land of good people], and the river *Rio du Cobre* [copper river]."

In March 1498, the viceroy of Mozambique boarded Vasco da Gama's ship as it lay in port along the east coast of Africa. The Portuguese presented him with small gifts, which he considered inadequate for a man of his esteemed position.

were many of the communities the fleet had previously encountered. It was an important trade center, host to merchants from Africa, Arabia, and India. Muslim merchants dressed in the finest robes of linen or cotton and wore *toucas*, or silk caps embroidered in gold. Lying in port when da Gama arrived were four Muslim vessels loaded with "gold, silver, cloves, pepper, ginger, silver rings . . . also quantities of pearls, jewels, and rubies"—all of the things the Portuguese had hoped to find.

Now it became Fernand Martins's duty to interpret. The Muslim sheik, or viceroy of the city, came aboard da Gama's ship and was presented with small gifts, including several *marlotas*, a Portuguese outfit made of silk or wool. The viceroy was accustomed to far richer tribute and made it plain that he scorned such small offerings.

At first the Muslims thought the Portuguese visitors were Turks or Moors from an unknown land. But when it was discovered they were Christians, tensions arose. Da Gama realized he must act with caution, for the size of his crew had seriously dwindled due to the many deaths caused by scurvy. On March 10 the captain-major ordered his ships to stand farther from the coast to prevent a possible attack. However, when water supplies ran low, men had to be sent ashore to restock them. They were driven off and threatened with serious consequences if they dared return. Da Gama, never long on patience, was enraged. Later, he took revenge, but it would be innocent people who would bear the brunt of his wrath.

THREE

Do Not Go Ashore!

By April 7, 1498, da Gama's fleet lay at anchor near Mombasa, on the coast of modern-day Kenya. Mombasa reminded the Portuguese of home. The "whitewashed stone houses had windows and terraces like those of the Peninsula [of Spain and Portugal]," a sight that made the sailors homesick. However, da Gama was not lured by Mombasa's charms, "for he was already suspicious . . . and anchored outside."

The local sheik sent gifts to the visitors—"a sheep, large quantities of oranges, lemons, and sugar cane, together with a ring as a pledge of security." The gifts came with a promise: If the captain-major wished to come ashore he would be supplied with "everything which he required." Da Gama responded with an inappropriate gift—a single string of inexpensive coral beads. He further insulted the Muslims by choosing two of his convict-sailors to deliver them, rather than ranking

Vasco da Gama was a respected leader. During the many trials
faced on his journeys to India, the hearty explorer
never expected his crew to endure anything he
wasn't willing to face himself.

officers. Nevertheless, the convicts were treated hospitably and given corn, cloves, and pepper when they returned to the fleet.

Da Gama's suspicions about Mombasa proved to be accurate, for it was later discovered that orders had been given "to capture us as soon as we entered the port." Around midnight on April 10, 1498, three days after their arrival, two *almadias*, or dugout canoes, carrying many men, approached the *São Raphael* and the *Berrio*. In the darkness, the men slipped into the water and began to cut the anchor ropes of the Portuguese ships. The sailors on watch mistook the soft splashing sounds for fish jumping out of the water and delayed sounding an alarm. When the culprits were discovered, they swam back to their dugouts and vanished in the night. "These and other wicked tricks were practiced upon us by these dogs," the author of the *Roteiro* wrote indignantly, "but our Lord did not allow them to succeed, because they were unbelievers."

In spite of the treachery of the Mombasans, da Gama rested his fleet offshore a few more days. It meant that he was able to take some hostages, which he did partly for revenge and partly to acquire bargaining tools to use later. At daybreak on April 14, when two *barcas*, or small cargo vessels, were sighted, the Portuguese gave swift chase. One boat, carrying seventeen passengers as well as gold, silver, and a load of corn, was seized.

The occupants of the *barca*, which included an elderly Muslim "of distinction" and his young wife, leaped into the water and tried to escape. But all of the Mombasans were captured and dragged aboard a Portuguese vessel. Then da Gama set sail. At sunset the same day, the Portuguese anchored at Malindi, about 30 leagues, or 90 miles (145 km) north of Mombasa.

Malindi, snugly located in a sheltered bay, was as attractive as Mombasa, boasting "lofty and well white-washed houses" surrounded

A Fateful Legacy

As the Portuguese traveled farther up the east coast of Africa and approached their longed-for destination—India—they came across more politically and economically complex communities. Yet "in meeting this challenge, da Gama displayed some of his weaknesses: a quick, violent temper, a lack of tact and judgment, and an insensate [brutal] cruelty. These were destined to affect the fortunes of his country in both Africa and Asia, and they laid the foundation of suspicion, mistrust, and fear which dogged the footsteps of his successors for centuries."

by palm groves and large fields of corn and vegetables. No welcoming party rowed out from shore, though, for officials had already gotten word that the Portuguese had taken seventeen prisoners at their previous stop.

The following morning, Easter Sunday 1498, the Muslims who had been captured told da Gama news he was most pleased to hear. There would be Christians from India in Malindi, along with everything else that he would need to continue his voyage—wood, water, and food. More importantly, a Christian probably could be hired as a navigator to help him get to India.

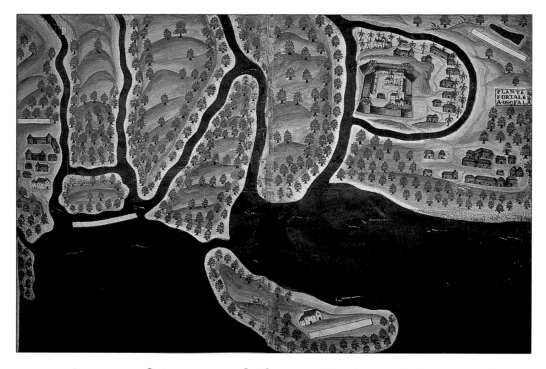

Early maps of the coasts of Africa and India and their nearby
islands were often drawn by men who had not even explored them.
The lack of accurate geographic information made Vasco da Gama's
task even more difficult. This map, made in the 1600s,
shows part of the coast of east Africa.

Da Gama ordered that the elderly Muslim who had been captured be taken ashore to explain to the local king that the Portuguese intentions were peaceful. Along with messengers from the local ruler, the man returned in a *zavra*—a small open vessel, sharp at the stern, with a square sail of matting that in modern times is called a dhow. They brought a peace offering of three fat sheep.

The king's messengers reported that he was eager to pursue friendly relations with the visitors. In return, da Gama sent back more appropriate gifts than he had at Mombasa—"two strings of coral, three wash-hand basins . . . and two pieces of lambel," or striped cotton fabric that was a highly prized trade item in Africa. A day later, the king sent six more sheep, together with "quantities of cloves, cumin, ginger, nutmeg and pepper," and suggested a face-to-face meeting. Best of all, he promised to provide da Gama with a navigator.

When the king's *zavra* later came alongside da Gama's vessel, the captain-major boarded the smaller craft, and friendly greetings were exchanged. The king of Malindi wore a cloak of damask trimmed with green satin and a richly decorated *touca*. He reclined on a bronze chair covered with cushions and was shaded from the sun by an umbrella of crimson satin. A servant wearing a sword in a silver sheath attended him, and musicians played on *anafils*, carved ivory trumpets as tall as they were. The king invited da Gama to his home to rest properly.

Da Gama, ever cautious, declined with a clever lie. He told the king that regretfully he was "not permitted by his master [the king of Portugal] to go on land, and if he were to do so a bad report would be given of him." However, he emphasized that he needed navigators to help him get to India, then softened his refusal to come ashore by releasing the seventeen Muslims he had captured at Mombasa. The king of Malindi was delighted, declaring "he valued this act more highly than if he had been presented with a town." To celebrate, the king sailed victory laps around da Gama's ship, while the Portuguese responded by firing their bombards.

On Thursday, April 19, four days after his Easter arrival, da Gama and Nicolas Coelho armed themselves and rowed closer to shore in longboats. The king came to the water's edge and once again pleaded with da Gama to come ashore. He explained that his "helpless father" was most eager to meet the explorer and offered to send his own sons out to board the *São Gabriel* to be kept as hostages to guarantee the captain-major's safety. Da Gama again declined the invitation.

When some Indians aboard trading vessels in Malindi's harbor visited Paulo's ship, they saw an altarpiece depicting the Virgin with the infant Jesus in her arms. They immediately knelt to pray before

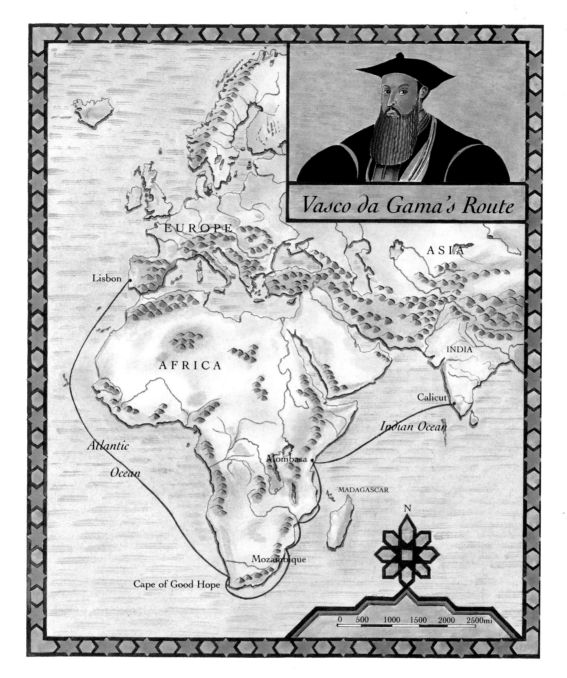

Vasco da Gama's Route

it, which convinced the Portuguese they were Christians. They wore "but little clothing . . . [and] told us that they ate no beef." Although some west coast Indians had been converted to Christianity centuries before, it is likely that the visitors were actually Hindus, not Christians, and mistook the image of the Virgin and Child as a goddess from their own religion. Before departing, the visitors warned da Gama, do not go ashore! No matter what the king of Malindi had promised, they whispered, it did not come from goodwill.

Da Gama turned the warning over in his mind. He'd been in the harbor for a week, yet the navigator the king had promised had yet to appear. It seemed clear that a simple request wasn't enough. He would have to be more forceful. When the king sent a special messenger to da Gama's ship, the man was held hostage until the promised navigator was sent aboard. The king realized he had been tricked, and a navigator, Ahmad ibn Majid, was duly delivered.

Before releasing his hostages, da Gama invited Majid to his cabin to assess the man's abilities. He skillfully demonstrated his familiarity with all aspects of navigation and da Gama was "much pleased," satisfied that he had gotten the services of a master.

There was no need to stay in Malindi any longer. The Portuguese crew was rested. Supplies of fruits and vegetables had already cured some cases of scurvy. Water casks were filled. Wood had been taken on board. As the fleet left port on Tuesday, April 24, 1498, the wind filled the ships' sails, clearly displaying the bold red crosses painted on them.

The fleet sailed for twenty-three days and covered an estimated 600 leagues, about 1,800 miles (2,900 km), without sighting land. By night, the constellation of Orion, the Great Bear, and the North Star were now visible—welcome sights, for they hadn't been seen in months. The monsoon (from the Arab word *mawsim*, meaning "time" or "season") period of high winds and rain had begun and provided the fleet with steady progress to the southwest.

RICHEST DID NOT MEAN MOST BEAUTIFUL

Being the richest city on the Indian coast didn't guarantee that Calicut had a beautiful harbor. Houses thatched with palm leaves pushed up to the ocean's edge like survivors on a raft. Monkeys swung noisily through the trees. Poisonous snakes were a common threat because Indian religious belief forbade killing them. Muddy banks above the shallow water reeked of filth. Crocodiles patrolled the shore, menacing man and beast alike. The harbor was so shallow that large ships were forced to lie at anchor off shore, as the Portuguese did. Only smaller vessels could sail in closer.

Nevertheless, warehouses along the seafront were filled with silk from China; finely woven Indian cotton; cloves, nutmeg, and peppers; mountains of oranges, lemons, mangoes, and bananas; and piles of ivory from the interior of India. Arrack, a drink made from the sap of palm trees, was sold by vendors in Calicut's narrow streets. The city was crowded with people from many nations—Arabia, Syria, China, Ceylon. And over everything lingered the perfume of fresh roses—"These people could not live without roses . . . they look on them as quite as necessary as food."

When land was finally sighted, heavy rain prevented Majid from positively identifying the coast. On the evening of May 20, 1498, however, he uttered the words da Gama had waited almost a year to hear, "We have arrived. . . . Here is the land where you desired to go." After almost eleven months the Portuguese fleet anchored off the southwestern coast of India, near the famous Malabar Coast—a few miles from Calicut, the richest and most important city in that part of the world.

Calicut was ruled by a *samorin*, a Sanskrit word meaning "lord of the sea," which in the Portuguese language became *zamorin*. As tactless as ever, da Gama sent one of his convict-sailors ashore to gather information. When the man was asked by Indian officials, "What brought you hither?" he candidly replied that his master came in search of Christians and spices. The convict was treated to a meal of bread and honey, then sent back to the fleet, accompanied by a Moor who, to the surprise of the Portuguese, spoke their own language. "A lucky venture!" he exclaimed. "Plenty of rubies, plenty of emeralds! You owe great thanks to God, for having brought you to a country holding such riches!" Da Gama must have smiled. More than Christians, it was wealth he had come so far to find.

F O U R

Prisoners in Paradise

When told to drop anchor in Calicut, a wary da Gama moved farther from shore, because "we . . . did not feel comfortable," noted the author of the *Roteiro*. The fleet was visited by a *wali*, or chief of police. The *wali* rowed out from the shore to da Gama's ship accompanied by 200 armed guards. They had been sent to escort da Gama safely to the palace of the *zamorin*, the *wali* announced through an interpreter.

The following morning, Monday, May 28, 1498, da Gama picked thirteen men, including the author of the *Roteiro*, to accompany him. Paulo was left in charge of the fleet, while Nicolas Coelho was instructed to wait near the shore with skiffs until the royal visit was over. Da Gama's instincts told him to be cautious, and he made arrangements with Paulo that if anything befell him and the thirteen others, no rescue attempt should be made. Instead, the fleet must immediately set sail for Portugal.

"We put on our best attire, placed bombards in our boats, and took with us trumpets and many flags," the *Roteiro* reads. "The reception was friendly, as if the people were pleased to see us, though at first appearances [they] looked threatening, for they carried naked swords in their hands. A palanquin [a chair carried on the shoulders of bearers] was provided for the captain-major, such as is used . . . by men of distinction."

The first stop was at the home of an official, where a meal of buttered rice and fish was provided. Then the Portuguese were rowed 2 miles (3.2 km) up the Elatur River to visit what they understood to be a Christian church. However, the tile-roofed, stone pagoda didn't look like the kind of church they had ever seen.

> *We did not go within the chapel, for it is the custom that only certain servants of the church, called quafees [priests] should enter. They threw holy water over us, and gave us some white earth [a mixture of dust, cow dung, sacrificial ash, sandalwood, and rice water], which the Christians of this country are in the habit of putting on their foreheads, breasts, around the neck and on the forearms.*

An hour before sunset, da Gama and his men arrived at the palace of the *zamorin*. They entered a "courtyard of great size," then passed through a series of doors leading to a smaller court where the king sat on a velvet couch beneath a golden canopy. He held a large gold cup into which he threw the husks of *tambur* (betel nuts), "which is chewed by the people of this country because of its soothing effects." It also stained their teeth a brownish color, giving their smiles an unsettling appearance. The king ordered water, with which the guests could wash their hands, then offered them fruit to eat.

When asked where he'd come from and why, da Gama explained that he was an ambassador from the king of Portugal, who believed there were Christian rulers in India with whom he wished to establish

Calicut was one of the richest ports in the East. Its crowded streets included traders from Persia, Syria, China, and Ceylon as well as every part of India itself. When Vasco da Gama and his men arrived, they saw elephants (upper right) for the first time, an animal unknown to Europeans at the time.

relations. The *zamorin*, listening through an interpreter, seemed friendly and smiled often at his guests. The talks continued late into the evening.

At last da Gama was asked if he wished to spend the night with Christians or Moors. The captain-major replied he preferred the company of the comrades he had come ashore with. However, a heavy monsoon rainstorm had come up, filling the streets with water and making it necessary for the Portuguese to lodge with one of the king's advisors. It was the beginning of what turned out to be a long, nerve-wracking ordeal.

CHRISTIAN SAINTS OR PAGAN GODS?

When the Portuguese visited the Indian "chapel" in Calicut, they saw Hindu worshippers kneeling and chanting, "Maria! Maria!" which they assumed was praise for the Virgin Mary. The hopes of King Manuel had been realized—there were, indeed, Christians in India. However, da Gama and his men were probably filled with doubt upon closer observation. The portraits on the stone walls were not of familiar Christian saints. Actually, some were images of the Hindu god Krishna and his mother Devaki Gauri, "the white goddess." Later, the Portuguese learned that the Hindus' chant, "Maria! Maria!" didn't refer to the Blessed Virgin, but to one of their own deities, Mari, or Mariamma, who was feared and honored as the goddess of smallpox.

The ruler of Calicut had seemed friendly initially, but the following day as da Gama assembled the gifts he intended to present to the *zamorin*—twelve pieces of *lambrel*, six wash basins, four scarlet hoods, four strings of coral, as well as cases of oil and honey—his Muslim host ridiculed them. The Portuguese were informed that the *zamorin* was accustomed to receiving gold and gems even from lower-class merchants. Much more was expected from an ambassador of the rich ruler

Vasco da Gama arrived in Calicut in May 1498, after a sea voyage of almost a year. The city, ruled by a zamorin, or king, was overflowing with what the Portuguese had come so far to find—gold, jewels, spices, and silks.

of a distant land. Da Gama didn't want to convey the impression that the king of Portugal was stingy, and he explained that the unsuitable gifts had been unwisely chosen by him, not by the king.

For two days da Gama was detained, permitted neither to take his gifts to the *zamorin* nor to return to his fleet. Had it dawned on him yet that he was a prisoner in a paradise of gold, emeralds, and rubies? He grew impatient, considered bursting in on the *zamorin* without permission, then thought better of acting recklessly. Meanwhile, his men weren't as concerned and were allowed to wander about the city. Among the fascinating sights they observed were elephants hauling a damaged ship onto the beach for repairs.

A MUSLIM WARNING TO THE ZAMORIN

Da Gama's problem in dealing with the *zamorin* was caused in part by his own miscalculation. To impress the *zamorin* with the power of the Portuguese, he told the ruler of Calicut that storms at sea had separated his ships from a much larger Portuguese fleet. He added that his voyage had taken two years. However, the swift progress of da Gama's fleet up the African coast had already been noted by Muslim merchants, who recognized how their own profits in India would be affected if the Portuguese were successful. The merchants advised the *zamorin* that da Gama was nothing but a liar and a common pirate who wanted only to rob them. They reported that the Portuguese had "fallen upon Mozambique with their hostile arms" and had created havoc in Mombasa. "If with so small a force they dare show the ferocity [brutality] of their disposition, what will they not perpetrate [commit] when they have great strength?" The Muslims cautioned, "if you do not immediately exert yourself . . . in a few years not only your crown but your life will be in the greatest jeopardy from a people so covetous, so ambitious, so warlike."

On May 30 da Gama and Fernando Martins were escorted again to the palace. Once there, they were kept waiting several hours. Finally they were greeted rudely and admitted to see the *zamorin*. You say you come from a rich country, the *zamorin* taunted, but you have brought me no valuable gifts! In any case, what do you have in your country that I might desire?

"Much corn, cloth, iron [and] bronze," da Gama replied, and suggested that he be allowed to return to his fleet to get samples of such products. The *zamorin* countered with his own suggestion: da Gama ought to anchor his ships, unload all of his merchandise,

Vasco da Gama explains to the ruler of Calicut that he has come as an ambassador, or representative, of King Manuel I of Portugal and that he hopes to establish friendly relations. For nearly three months, however, da Gama and his men were held prisoner.

47

HOW ELEPHANTS WERE CAPTURED

India was a land of many animals unfamiliar to most Europeans, the most majestic of which were elephants. The author of the *Roteiro* explained how these beasts were captured in the Indian jungles. A tame female elephant was led out to a path frequented by wild elephants. Then a large, deep pit was dug in the path and hidden with brush. The female, docile and obedient to human command, was left tethered along the trail. Soon, a wild elephant, its curiosity aroused by the presence of the stranger, stumbled unwarily

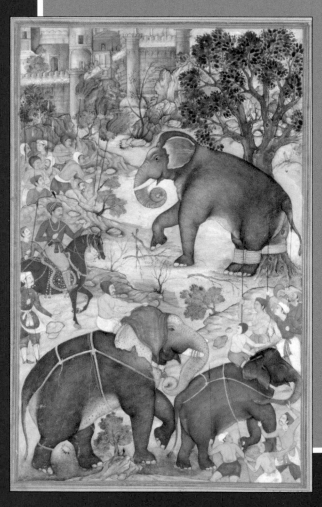

into the hole, which was too deep for it to climb out of unaided. For several days, it was left alone without food or water. Then small supplies were delivered, followed by a bit more each day for a month. The elephant became so tame "he all but learns to speak." Heavy chains were clamped to the animal's legs, then with the help of tame elephants it was hauled out of its prison. According to the *Roteiro*, the tamed elephants then were "kept in stables like horses."

and "sell it . . . to the best advantage." Without giving da Gama a chance to reply, the *zamorin* ended the discussion.

It grew dark on the way back to the coast, and da Gama and his men became separated. When they were reunited, they took a night's lodging in the home of a Muslim trader and were given a meal of chicken and rice. On the morning of June 1, 1498, da Gama demanded *almadias* to take him and his men out to the fleet.

Although it had been agreed that the Portuguese could return to their ships, their Muslim host "afforded . . . no opportunity for doing so, for [he] immediately closed all the doors, and many armed men came to guard us," reads the *Roteiro*. The Muslim demanded that da Gama take down his ships' sails and surrender their rudders. Da Gama refused to render his ships useless. If he and his men must stay and die of hunger, they would "bear it, as they cared nothing for that," he declared.

Days passed. Neither side yielded to the other. Finally, on June 24 the Portuguese goods were moved from the ships to the shore and sold. By twos and threes, sailors from da Gama's fleet came ashore on leave. On August 9, 1498, a gift of amber and coral was sent to the *zamorin*, accompanied by a message stating that the Portuguese now wished to sail for home. The *zamorin* scorned the simple gift but, prodded by the Muslim host, demanded payment of customs charges for the merchandise that had been sold.

Although da Gama was allowed back on board his ship, several of his crew who had taken leave remained on shore. In essence, they were prisoners of the *zamorin*. On Sunday, August 19, twenty-five officials came out from shore to negotiate with da Gama, including six men of high rank. The captain-major suspected that the Muslims intended to destroy the Portuguese ships and kill everyone aboard, so he took the high-ranking visitors and twelve others hostage. Da Gama sent the remaining negotiators back to shore with a message saying the hostages

This tapestry shows the Portuguese unloading a mythical beast, the unicorn, in Calicut. Although unicorns were not found in the East, as the artist presumed, horses and camels were unloaded from ships in this way, lowered in slings.

would be released only when his own men and the merchandise that hadn't been sold were returned.

One week later, seven boats came alongside the Portuguese ships. The men whose release da Gama had demanded were delivered, but not the merchandise. In retaliation, he released six hostages, but kept the others. When small boats arrived carrying the goods, da Gama refused to accept it. It no longer mattered, he shouted arrogantly, adding that he intended to keep the men he had captured. He also warned that when he returned to India he would teach the people of Calicut a lesson they wouldn't forget.

On Wednesday, August 29, 1498—having been virtual prisoners of the *zamorin* for three months—da Gama set sail for home. He and his men had been gone from Portugal for more than a year, and the history of the world had been set on a violent, new course.

FIVE

Admiral of the East Indian Seas

At noon the following day, while only about 3 miles (4.8 km) off the Indian coast, the wind dropped, and the sails of the Portuguese ships went limp. Immediately seventy boats, powered by oarsmen and filled with armed Muslims, surrounded da Gama's fleet. Da Gama ordered the bombards to be fired, but no sooner had he taken action than a sudden breeze filled the Portuguese sails again. Even so, boatloads of angry Muslims continued in pursuit, and only a sudden thunderstorm turned them back.

By September 20, in spite of "feeble winds," the fleet arrived at the Angediva Islands, where wood, water, and fresh vegetables were taken on board. As his men busied themselves with the supplies, da Gama noticed the approach of two large galleys. Taking them to be pursuers from Calicut, he ordered them fired upon. One of the vessels escaped, while the other was found to be carrying coconuts and palm

The Portuguese and the defenders of India waged vicious battles.
Atrocities were committed by both sides, but history indicates that
Vasco da Gama was particularly cruel.

sugar, not armed men. When the ship's Hindu owner offered to buy his vessel back for a large sum, da Gama could have accepted. But he refused and sank it instead.

Having frightened off their pursuers, the Portuguese remained at the Angedivas for twelve days, "eating much fish . . . [and] many pumpkins and cucumbers," before setting sail again. The voyage across the Arabian Sea to the east coast of Africa proved a long and terrible one. Due to unfavorable winds—or no winds at all—it lasted from October 2, 1498, until January 2, 1499. Supplies of fresh vegetables ran out. Barrels of water turned foul. Scurvy struck without mercy. Thirty men died (thirty had previously died on the voyage to Calicut). Only seven or eight men on each vessel were strong enough to manage the sails.

"I assure you that if this state of affairs had continued for another fortnight [two weeks], there would have been no men at all to navigate the ships," the author of the *Roteiro* noted. "Even iron-willed da Gama enforced obedience with difficulty . . . all bonds of discipline had gone."

On the evening of January 2, the port of Mogadishu on the upper east coast of Africa was sighted. But there was no way to be sure it was a safe place to drop anchor. Three days later, a storm damaged the *São Raphael*, and eight boatloads of pirates attacked the fleet, which was forced to push farther out to sea. On January 7, Malindi came into view, with its charming whitewashed houses and palm trees. The Portuguese were recognized from their previous visit and were given oranges, eggs, and several sheep. However, the food came too late to help the last victims of scurvy, who died in port.

The additional deaths made it obvious to da Gama that his crew was too small to sail all three ships—the *São Raphael*, the *São Gabriel*, and the *Berrio*—back to Portugal. On Sunday, January 13, while anchored off the coast of Mombasa, the contents and crew of the damaged *São Raphael* were transferred to the other two vessels, and then the ship was set afire and sunk. It was a sad moment for the da Gamas.

Paulo had commanded the *São Raphael* but had been ill for weeks and was not expected to live long enough to see his homeland again. Only the vessel's archangel figurehead was saved and can be seen today at the Church of the Jeronimos in Portugal.

By March 20, "the Lord gave us such a good wind that . . . we were able to double the Cape of Good Hope," the author of the *Roteiro* wrote. For the next twenty-seven days, the winds continued to be fair and swept the two remaining Portuguese ships—with Nicolas Coelho in command of the *Berrio*—up the west coast of the African continent to the familiar Cape Verde Islands.

The archangel figurehead was all that remained of the São Raphael, sunk in the waters off of eastern Africa.

LOVED BETTER THAN ALL ELSE

Da Gama had good reason to bless the strong winds because his brother Paulo had begun to cough up blood. His disease—tuberculosis—had reached a terminal stage. On the island of São Thiago, the captain-major put John da Sá in command of the *São Gabriel* then chartered a smaller vessel for himself and Paulo to travel more swiftly for Lisbon. But the ship could not sail fast enough to save him. It became clear that he was close to death—and being unwilling to cast his brother's body into the sea like a common sailor's—Vasco landed at Terceira, one of the islands that make up the Azores. One day after arriving in the third week of August 1499 (the precise date was not recorded), Paulo da Gama died, *como muyto bô Christâo que era*, "like the good Christian he was." He was buried at the monastery of St. Francis. Paulo's death left Vasco "numb with grief." Da Gama—not easily given to emotion—had loved his brother "better than all else in the world."

Coelho sailed into Lisbon harbor on July 10, 1499, but da Gama, mourning Paulo's death, didn't arrive until August 29. In a sense, da Gama's mission had been a failure. He hadn't established good trade relations in India due to the treachery of Muslim merchants and his own high-handed behavior. Of approximately 170 seamen who began the voyage, only 55 came back alive. "God gave the Portuguese a small land for their birth place," it was said, "but all the world to die in," which proved true for da Gama's crew.

Yet there was no denying what he had accomplished. He had discovered the sea route to India and commanded the first fleet of any European nation to enter Indian ports. He had completed a two-year voyage covering more than 6,000 miles (9,600 km). Most importantly, "What he had accomplished could be repeated, for the first step is always the most difficult." And it was repeated—not only by other Portuguese, but eventually by Vasco himself.

Da Gama returned to a hero's welcome. He had fulfilled the goals that Prince Henry had set for Portugal and more than justified the confidence King Manuel had placed in him. When da Gama dropped anchor, the king sent nobles from the royal court to accompany the explorer to the palace.

On September 8, 1499, the streets of Lisbon were crowded with citizens who were eager to catch a glimpse of da Gama. They wanted to see the returning hero not only because he had "done such a great thing" as reaching India by sea but also because "everyone thought that he was dead." Da Gama's appearance must have been bizarre, for he hadn't trimmed his black beard or hair since leaving the same harbor two years and two months earlier! But King Manuel wasn't stingy with either words of praise or with rewards. Although da Gama still mourned the loss of his brother, King Manuel's greeting must have been a comfort to his spirit, for it paid homage to Paulo as well as to himself.

"Console yourself for the death of your brother," the king urged. "Although [he] has died, his affairs shall not suffer by closing the [rewards] which I would have made him had he been alive." Nor would the families of the many others who died on the voyage be ignored, for the king promised that "it shall be the same for all those who died as for those who have remained alive."

With its success in taming the high seas, Portugal's influence could be felt in distant parts of the world once thought unreachable. This decorative plate combines elements of two cultures brought into closer contact as a result of Portugal's exploration. In the center is a sturdy Portuguese ship surrounded by designs typical of Islamic art of the era.

Da Gama was awarded the title of admiral of the East Indian seas. The king also took the opportunity to give himself a grand title—king, by the grace of God, of Portugal and of the Algarves, both on this side of the sea and beyond it in Africa, lord of Guinea and of the conquest, navigation, and commerce of Ethiopia, Arabia, Persia, and India.

Da Gama's return caused much anxiety in several European nations, especially Italy. For more than two centuries, the Italian cities of Genoa and Venice had derived their great wealth from trade with the East. "As soon as the news . . . reached Venice," wrote a fifteenth-century observer, "the populace was thunderstruck, and the wiser among them regarded [it] as the worst they could have received." It

As a boy of seven, Henry the Navigator had been Vasco da Gama's hero. Later in life, da Gama held it among his greatest honors that he was the man who realized the prince's dream of finding a sea route to India.

BRAGGING RIGHTS

Even before da Gama rode triumphantly through the streets of Lisbon, King Manuel made sure that the king and queen of Spain were aware of the Portuguese accomplishment. In July 1499, he wrote to Queen Isabella and King Ferdinand, who had taken smug satisfaction in Columbus's discovery, to assert bragging rights of his own. "Vasco da Gama, a nobleman of our household, and his brother Paulo da Gama, with four vessels . . . did reach India and other kingdoms and lordships bordering it," King Manuel declared, "finding large cities . . . and great populations, among whom is carried on all the trade in spices and precious stones which are forwarded . . . to Mecca [by the Moors], and thence to Cairo, whence they are dispersed throughout the world. Of these spices . . . they have brought a quantity, including cinnamon, cloves, ginger, nutmeg, and pepper . . . also many fine stones of all sorts, such as rubies . . . they also came to a country in which there are mines of gold." King Manuel added pointedly that there would now be "an opportunity for destroying the Moors of those parts." The stage was set for more bloody conflict between Muslims and Christians, which had already raged for centuries.

was obvious that the great centers of commerce would be transferred from Italian-controlled harbors in the Mediterranean to Portuguese-controlled ports along the Atlantic.

No one could deny that Vasco da Gama was a great explorer. He was also a man of great courage. He was willing to bear hardships along with his men. He was calm and level headed in the face of danger. Yet he was also quite greedy.

For him, enough was never quite enough. He wasn't entirely satisfied with what King Manuel had given him and asked for sovereignty, or control, over his birthplace at Sines. His ties to the place ran deep. He had spent his boyhood there, and his father had been the *alcaide-mór* of the village.

However, Sines already belonged to the powerful duke of Coimbra. Nevertheless, on Christmas Eve 1499, the king signed a document granting da Gama all "the privileges, revenues, and taxes" from the town. The duke, an influential man in his own right, was not pleased and refused to give up his property. Manuel was forced to take back his offer to da Gama and placated him with more money.

Vasco da Gama, now forty years old, had honors and wealth to spare. It was time to rest and to marry, and he did both. Catharina de Athayde, the attractive young daughter of a noble family, became his bride in 1499 in the village of Évora. Their long marriage produced one daughter, Izabel, and six sons. Of da Gama's six sons, Francisco was the eldest and inherited da Gama's royal titles. Second-born Estavan became governor of India in 1540; Paulo was killed in a naval battle off the coast of Malacca in 1534; Christovan died in Abyssinia in 1542; Pedro was appointed captain of Malacca in 1541; the youngest, Alvaro, followed in Pedro's footsteps and also held the same title.

SIX

The Will of God, Not Men

King Manuel wasted no time sending a second, larger expedition to India. He asked da Gama to take command, but the explorer preferred to enjoy his new life, in which he became so wealthy that the Venetian ambassador to Portugal, Leonardo Masser, estimated that "only six princes of the Church could boast of larger incomes."

Command was then given to thirty-two-year-old Pedro Cabral, a surprising choice, for Cabral wasn't an experienced seaman. Bartolomeu Dias, the navigator who had sailed with da Gama, was also included in the expedition and supplied the know-how that Cabral lacked. On March 9, 1500, thirteen ships stocked with enough supplies to last a year and a half left Lisbon.

Da Gama had gone to India as an explorer; Cabral went as a conqueror. He had trained gunners aboard, as well as "Franciscan friars, and merchants under orders to buy and sell in the King's name." He also car-

In 1500 Pedro Cabral tried to retrace Vasco da Gama's route to India, but he sailed so far to the west that he dropped anchor off the coast of Brazil in South America, the first European to do so.

ried a letter to the *zamorin* warning that the Portuguese intentions now were "to follow the will of God rather than of men, and not to fail through any opposition."

Cabral's fleet followed da Gama's route and sailed so far to the west that, on April 22, 1500, anchors were dropped near the shores of what Cabral called *Terra da Santa Cruz*, "Land of the Holy Cross." The discovery of Brazil was accidental, yet the empire the Portuguese later established in South America made them far richer than their colonies in Asia.

While crossing the South Atlantic, the fleet was caught in a violent storm and four vessels were lost, among them the one commanded by Dias. Six months later, on September 13, 1500, Cabral arrived at Calicut.

The *zamorin*—alarmed by the threatening message that was delivered to him by da Gama—sent greetings of friendship and assigned living quarters and a warehouse along the shore for the Portuguese to use.

The Muslims, however, had their own plans. On December 16, 1500, under cover of darkness, several thousand Muslims surrounded the warehouse. A cry of "*Ladrões, ladrões!*" or "Thieves, thieves!" went up from the Portuguese, but it came too late. The Moors "put . . . its [the warehouse's] occupants to the sword," including thirty of the eighty Portuguese inside.

Cabral was outraged by the massacre. He bombarded the city, setting many of its wooden buildings on fire and burning ten Arab ships anchored near shore. He retreated to a neighboring port, Cochin, whose merchants, jealous of those in Calicut, eagerly struck a trade deal with the Portuguese. Cabral loaded his ships with as much cinnamon, pepper, cloves, musk, and Chinese silks and porcelain as they would hold and sailed for home on January 16, 1501.

Cabral entered Lisbon's harbor on July 31, 1501, a year and a half after his departure. Although he had lost several vessels, the profit on the Portuguese investment was 100 percent. King Manuel was so elated that he advised Italian guests at his court to come to Lisbon from now on to purchase the riches of the East. "In short he feels that he has India under his control," observed Giovanni Matteo Cretico of Venice.

In spite of his success, Cabral had a falling out with King Manuel. In irritation, the king called for da Gama and asked him to lead the next expedition. The king promised an even larger fleet—twenty ships in all. Ten were to be loaded with as many goods as they would hold, five to cruise the Indian Ocean to destroy any competition from the Moors, and five to be stationed along the African coast to protect the new Portuguese settlements that were to be established. Da Gama, refreshed by his two-year vacation, welcomed the invitation.

All in the Family

Lisbon had changed much in the four years since da Gama's departure in 1497. The streets were crowded with foreigners—Italian, German, French, Dutch, English, and Spanish—all eager to profit from trade, while at the same time keeping a jealous eye on Portuguese expansion. Da Gama made sure his own relatives, not strangers, would profit from his voyage. So he divided command of his twenty ships among his family. He took control of the ten cargo vessels himself. His uncle Vicente Sodré commanded the five ships that were to destroy Muslim competitors. To Estavan da Gama, a nephew, was awarded control of the five ships whose duty it was to protect the settlements. It was a family affair, but critics called it what it was—nepotism, or using power to benefit friends and relatives.

By the late 1500s, Lisbon was a bustling sea port, much to the chagrin of Portugal's rivals, other European nations seeking their own share of the profitable trade with the East.

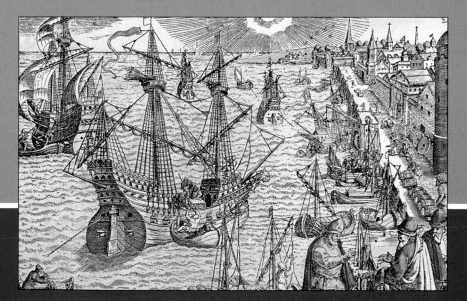

Although no *Roteiro*, or logbook, was kept of da Gama's second voyage, a Flemish sailor whose name has been lost to history, kept a record of the expedition entitled *Calcoen*, or Calicut. The journal consisted of names, dates, and places from which historians have gleaned a wealth of information. It was no surprise that a Dutchman would be traveling with da Gama. The Dutch were already trading in India by crossing through Egypt and had established themselves as powerful competitors throughout the East. A second source of information about the voyage comes from an account written by Thomé Lopes, a clerk on one of the ships commanded by Estavan da Gama.

Before da Gama's departure from Portugal on February 10, 1502, King Manuel celebrated Mass at the Cathedral of Lisbon. Alberto Cantino, a diplomat who was present, reported that da Gama wore "a long surtout [coat] of crimson satin of the French type, lined with ermine [fur], and a beret and tunic matched the surtout, and adorned with a neck chain of gold." Luxury had become as much a part of da Gama's life as it was the king's.

The first stop on the voyage was the Canary Islands, where provisions were replenished. On June 14, 1502, the fleet anchored off the east coast of Africa at Sofala (from the Arabic *saflá*, or "low ground"), noted for exporting gold mined in Africa's interior. One of the most unusual trading items to be found in port was hippopotamus teeth, considered more valuable than elephant ivory because they were whiter and harder.

When da Gama arrived at the island of Kilwa, he recalled that the local emir, or ruler, had refused Cabral's order to pledge submission to the king. Da Gama considered the refusal an insult and sent word that he intended to burn Kilwa to the ground if the emir didn't immediately agree. The man was no fool, and he quickly consented.

When da Gama's fleet anchored off Calicut on October 30, 1502, word of the Portuguese massacre of the 380 Muslim passengers aboard the *Meri* had already reached the *zamorin*. The *zamorin* realized he

THE DARK SIDE OF DOMINATION

Da Gama's new title, admiral of the East Indian seas—giving him all "the honors, preeminces, liberties, power, jurisdiction, revenues, privileges and rights" of his position—heightened his own sense of self-righteousness. On October 1, 1502, the *Meri*, a ship carrying Muslim passengers home from a pilgrimage to Mecca was sighted along the coast of Malabar. The vessel also carried merchandise—enough, wrote Thomé Lopes, "to ransom every Christian slave in the kingdom of Fez." The Portuguese chased the ship, collecting 12,000 ducats from it as well as goods worth 10,000 ducats. However, da Gama didn't stop there. "The admiral set that ship ablaze with much cruelty and without the least pity, and it burned with every one aboard," said Thomé Lopes. Mothers stood on the blazing decks with their babies held high, begging for mercy. In the end, 380 men, women, and children perished in this act of ruthless brutality.

had made a mistake in treating da Gama rudely on the first expedition and hastily sent messengers to welcome the admiral. They were treated with contempt, however, for da Gama knew that this time he had the upper hand.

When a small fleet of fishermen drew alongside the admiral's vessels, intending to sell their catch to the Portuguese, da Gama seized thirty-eight of them. They were dragged on board and hanged in full view of those on shore. The men's bodies were hacked to pieces and thrown overboard to wash ashore with the tide. Messages written in Arabic were attached to some of the body parts, warning the citizens of Calicut that a similar fate awaited them. When he had been driven out of India two years earlier, da Gama had warned them that he would teach them all a lesson they would not forget.

On November 7, 1502, leaving six ships at Calicut to prevent other traders from entering the port, da Gama sailed to Cochin in search of spices and other merchandise. Just after the new year, on January 3, 1503, the *zamorin* sent a messenger, accompanied by his young son, to Cochin, inviting the admiral to return to Calicut and sign a peace agreement. As da Gama neared Calicut, he was surrounded by Arab ships and realized he had been lured into a trap.

This map, made in 1500, shows Calicut and the southern coast of India. Da Gama's journey to Asia greatly advanced European knowledge of and interest in the East.

Da Gama escaped but took swift revenge. He released the messenger but kept the man's young son. He hanged the boy from the yardarm, then sailed up and down Calicut's shore with the grisly memento on display.

The Portuguese had nearly finished loading in Cochin when word came that the Muslims, driven by their own desire for revenge, had organized a large fleet and planned to attack. Da Gama gathered all his ships and sailed back to Calicut for a showdown. On February 12, 1503, he easily defeated the Muslim armada. He lingered for eight days along the coast in case the Moors decided to attack again. With any threat dispelled, he then sailed for Portugal.

The voyage home was a long one. On April 20, "a contrary wind . . . blew us for five whole weeks [and] drove us 1,000 miles [1,609 km] out of our direct course . . . and there was a great tempest of rain, hail, snow, thunder, and lightning," wrote the Flemish sailor. At last, on October 11, 1503, da Gama dropped anchor in Lisbon. The voyage, which had taken twenty months, brought more gold to King Manuel and even greater glory to Vasco da Gama.

Da Gama, proud and greedy, was disappointed that he wasn't awarded everything he had expected after his second voyage. King Manuel did not want to give any of his subjects too much power, influence, or wealth. He had had a falling out with Cabral; now, the same thing happened with da Gama. The admiral had expected that Sines would at last become his. When it didn't, he simply moved his family there and acted as if it had.

The duke of Coimbra complained to King Manuel, forcing the king to issue a decree on March 21, 1507, ordering the entire da Gama family to leave Sines within thirty days and forbidding their return. If the decree was violated, da Gama would be fined and certain punishments would be "meted out to those who do not obey the command of their king and lord."

The Will of God, Not Men

To be driven out of the town of his birth like a common *degredado*, or criminal, was a bitter humiliation for da Gama. The king attempted to soothe the explorer's wounded feelings by giving him additional grants and payments, special hunting privileges, properties in India, and exemption from various Portuguese taxes. Da Gama moved to Évora, built a house, and isolated himself from public life. Only one thing could mollify him—to be called back into service by the king.

A TRAIL OF FIRE AND BLOOD

In the wake of his second voyage, da Gama left "a broad trail of fire, blood, and hatred . . . the blood of innocents, needlessly shed, and of hatreds that could have been avoided by the exercise of tact, patience, and prudence." Those who came after da Gama inherited this legacy, and eventually the Portuguese were stripped of everything they'd won. That other great Portuguese explorer, Ferdinand Magellan, had once been described as "the devil entered into a Portuguese." The same assessment could easily be made of Vasco da Gama.

Manuel I was only twenty-four years old when he became king of Portugal in 1495. He supported the exploration of Africa's coast and chose Vasco da Gama as the leader of an expedition to do so.

The call never came. In 1518 da Gama, tired of waiting, offered his services to other nations. A year earlier, in October 1517, Magellan had done the same thing by selling his skills to the king of Spain. Consequently, King Manuel's response to da Gama's decision was stern: "We command you to remain in our kingdom until the end of December of this year [1518], and we hope that by that time you will have seen the error which you are committing, and that you will desire to serve us as is befitting, and not to take the extreme step which you propose."

King Manuel sought other ways to appease da Gama. One of the king's nephews, the duke of Bragança, agreed to give up his control of the town of Vidigueira along with his title of count. An agreement was signed at Évora on November 7, 1519, giving the property and title to da Gama, "irrevocable [not reversible] for all time." Four days after Christmas 1519, the admiral became Count da Gama of Vidigueira. It was not Sines, but it was better than nothing.

The king of Portugal was not pleased when some of his greatest navigators began selling their services to foreign powers. King Ferdinand and Queen Isabella of Spain were more than happy to tap the talents of their successful neighbor to the west.

King Manuel's rule was about to come to an end. In the autumn of 1521, a plague descended on Portugal and caught the king in its wake. On December 13 after an illness of nine days, Manuel died and was succeeded by his oldest son. John III "rode to his coronation mounted on a handsome gray horse," and it was he—a boy of only nineteen—who finally called Vasco da Gama back to serve his country.

S E V E N

So Strong a Spirit

In the nearly quarter-century after da Gama had left India, officials who had been sent there to govern Portugal's distant empire enjoyed an easy, affluent life. Far from Lisbon and the watchful eye of King Manuel, they pleased themselves on the one hand and governed poorly on the other. When King John III assumed the Portuguese throne, however, the situation changed.

In spite of his youth, King John was determined to stop corruption in the colonies. He was aware that profits that should have been going into the Portuguese treasury often ended up in private pockets. He also knew it would take a ruthless enforcer of discipline to put things right. Who better than Vasco da Gama?

On February 24, 1524, da Gama, the count of Vidigueira, swore allegiance to the new king and accepted the title viceroy of India. Although now sixty-four years old, the father of seven children, and a wealthy man,

John III, the eldest son of Manuel I, became king of Portugal in 1521. It was he who called da Gama back into service on behalf of the crown. Da Gama and King John's father had had a disagreement over the tribute the explorer was due after his successful passages to India.

the invitation to serve Portugal again was irresistible. Mindful as always of the welfare of his heirs, da Gama made sure that in the event of his death his new title would be inherited by his eldest son, Francisco.

On April 9, 1524, with a fleet of fourteen vessels and 3,000 men, da Gama boarded the *St. Catherine of Mount Sinai* and sailed from the harbor in Lisbon to take up his new post. Accompanying him were Estavan, his second-born son, and third-born Paulo, named in honor of the brother da Gama had buried twenty-five years earlier on the island of Terceira.

Before their departure, the new viceroy lectured his crew about sneaking their wives and sweethearts aboard, "on account of the quarrels and plots" that would occur if some men had female companionship, while others did not. "Any woman . . . found in the ships . . . would be flogged [whipped] publicly, even though she were married," he warned. At Mozambique, three women were discovered and handed over to da Gama. He ordered them locked up until the fleet arrived in the Portuguese colony of Goa in India.

Getting to India wasn't any easier than it had been the first or second time. After leaving Mozambique, violent storms sank three vessels, and everyone aboard was lost. The crew of a fourth ship mutinied, murdered its captain, took command of the vessel, and turned to piracy. Scurvy and beriberi broke out on the remaining ships, causing the loss of yet more men.

Then, early on the morning of September 8, 1524, as the ships lay becalmed, stranded without wind to fill the sails, off the Indian coast near Dabul, the sea began to boil like water over a brisk fire. The vessels pitched violently, tumbling cargo and crew all about. A physician aboard one ship explained that the disturbance—lasting about one hour, including aftershocks—was the result of an underwater earthquake. The only death occurred when a sailor, crazed with fear, jumped overboard and drowned.

The incident frightened da Gama's crew, but the new viceroy was quick to turn the occasion to his own advantage. "Friends, rejoice and be happy," he urged, "for even the sea trembles before us."

A few days later, da Gama was welcomed at the port city of Goa (from the Hindu word *gomant*, meaning "district of cowherds"), near Calicut. Affonso d'Albuquerque had conquered the city in 1510, boasting to King Manuel that he had massacred 6,000 Muslim men, women, and children in the process.

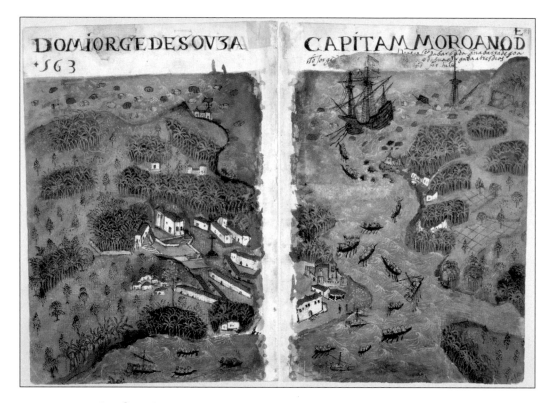

Goa, north of Calicut, became the Portuguese capital in India. From its harbor, the Portuguese dominated the trade in gold, silver, spices, and gems, all of which were in great demand by European nations. This strict trade control allowed Portugal to become the richest nation of the era.

When da Gama arrived, however, Portuguese colonists as well as the native population eagerly turned out to greet him. They believed his appointment meant a change in the city's fortunes, which had been badly managed under Governor Duarte de Menezes, a man famous for his greed. Portuguese observer Gaspar Correa, who had lived in India for many years, witnessed da Gama's arrival. Da Gama recognized that the best way to impress his new subject was to demonstrate his greatness. He intended to make a grand impression, and he did.

A Threat Is Carried Out

The three women that da Gama had imprisoned at Mozambique were the first in Goa to experience his anger. Before leaving home, he had warned his crew that wives or sweethearts who had been smuggled aboard would be publicly flogged, that "never shall they meet with anything from me except all severity and punishment." There should have been no doubt he meant it. Many officials, bishops, and the Brothers of Mercy interceded on behalf of the women, but da Gama was unmoved. Each of the women had to endure 200 lashes, administered in public.

Correa wrote, "[Da Gama] was served by men bearing silver maces [clubs], by a major-domo [a butler], and two pages with gold neck chains, many equerries [officers in charge of horses] and body servants. . . . He had a guard of two hundred men, with gilt pikes . . . [and] kept a splendid table." In short, he arrived like a king. Correa astutely noted something else: "He was a very disdainful man, ready to anger, very rash, much feared and respected, very knowing and experienced in all matters."

Many of the viceroy's first acts in India were highly practical. He ordered the repair of the walls around the city, in which "he took much pleasure," observed Correa. Horses were vital to the defense of the city, and 1,343 were brought in from the Persian Gulf city of Ormuz (36 of the animals died along the way). Under the former governor, Menezes, the king's officers had been selling artillery to local merchants, then pocketing the money themselves. Da Gama ordered that all such property be returned within thirty days under penalty of death. The hospital was filled not with sick persons who needed care, but with men who used it as a hotel. They were promptly evicted. To maintain order on shore, sailors aboard ships in the harbor were denied shore leave.

Not long after arriving at his new post, it became clear that da Gama was ill. Had he known he was ill before leaving Portugal? Perhaps, which might have been one of the reasons he so shrewdly saw to his oldest son's inheritance before he left. His age, the heat, and the aggravation of dealing with Menezes did nothing to improve his health. Nevertheless, he left Goa and traveled to Cochin to talk there with Portuguese officials.

Meantime, Menezes snatched up as much wealth as he could lay his hands on. According to Correa, Menezes had a chest full of "rich gold stuffs, pearls, and jewelry . . . worth a large price," which he

Even in later years, when Vasco da Gama's hair had turned gray,
the explorer's eyes still possessed the piercing, hawklike quality
that intimidated friends and foes alike.

buried on the beach when he was called to Cochin to meet with da Gama. Menezes was pleased to discover that the new viceroy was ill and thought that if da Gama died he might resume his old post as well as his greedy habits.

Da Gama began to suffer "great pains in the neck," wrote Correa, and large boils prevented him from turning his head in any direction. Modern physicians wonder if the condition—well known in ancient times—was caused by anthrax, an infectious disease in cattle and sheep that can be transmitted to people. Da Gama was moved from the fortress in Cochin where he had been staying to the home of a Portuguese official, Diogo Pereira, where he could receive better care.

The viceroy—not a patient man in the best of times—was given to fits of irritation. There was so much work that needed to be done. He worked tirelessly, foregoing his usual afternoon nap. As his health worsened, he was forced to take to his bed, from which he continued to issue orders, receive reports, and consult with administrators. Soon, however, his condition prevented him from speaking. It became obvious the end was near.

Da Gama prayed to his patron saint, Saint Anthony, and called for his son Estavan—one of the few persons whom he trusted completely—and gave him reports to deliver to King John III. He directed that all his servants be paid what was owed them and that his clothing and furnishings be donated to the city's churches and hospital. Among da Gama's final decisions was a surprising act of forgiveness: A sum of money was given to each of the women who had been publicly flogged for hiding on board his ship.

The man who fulfilled Prince Henry's dream of finding a sea road to India was prepared for death. It came on the morning of Christmas Eve 1524, a scant three months after his return to India.

He was buried at the monastery chapel of St. Anthony in Cochin, with orders that his remains be returned to Portugal at a future date. Correa observed, "It pleased the Lord to give this man so strong a spirit, that without any human fear he passed through so many perils . . . during the discovery of India."

In 1539, fifteen years after his death, da Gama's bones were returned to Portugal and laid to rest in the Church of Our Lady of the Relics of Vidigueira. His eldest son, Francisco, then the second count of Vidigueira, established a fund to guarantee that a daily Mass would be said for his father. When a new church was built in Vidigueira in 1593, the explorer's coffin was placed in the new chapel. The words, "Here lies the great argonaut [adventurer] Dom Vasco da Gama, First Count of Vidigueira, Admiral of the East Indies and their famous discoverer," were inscribed on the stone slab that covered the coffin.

In 1834, almost 240 years later, the Portuguese government suppressed various religious institutions in order to strengthen the power of civil (secular) government over ecclesiastical (church) government. Among them was the church at Vidigueira. After the church was abandoned, thieves vandalized the coffins of the dead, stole the valuables inside, and scattered the bones about. In 1871 historian Teixeria de Aragão urged the Portuguese government to remove da Gama's remains to a more suitable resting place.

Almost 383 years after he'd set out on his first voyage, da Gama's casket, along with the figurehead of Paulo's ship, the *São Raphael*, were transported to the Church of the Jerominos in Lisbon. On June 8, 1880, the explorer was laid to rest again. But da Gama had not yet finished his journey.

In 1898, on the 400-year anniversary of his departure from Portugal, his bones were reburied in the same small chapel at Restello

First buried in India, the body of Vasco da Gama was later moved to the Church of the Jeronimos near Lisbon.

where he had knelt in all-night prayer with his brother Paulo and the two other captains from his first voyage, Nicolas Coelho and Gonçalvo Álvares. Vasco da Gama's final resting place is a tomb supported by six crouching marble lions. The carved inscription, from Portugal's famous epic poem, *Os Lusiadas*, by Luís Vaz de Camões, eloquently recalled the beginning of the explorer's first voyage:

Partimos nos assi do sancto tempolo
Que nas praias do mar esta assentado.

Thus we departed from the holy church
Which on the margins of the sea is built.

Afterword

Goa, the city north of Calicut, was the capital of an empire the Portuguese called *Estado da India*, the State of India. Portugal went on to establish holdings in Ceylon (now called Sri Lanka), Macao, Japan, Brazil, and even forbidden kingdoms such as Tibet and Vietnam.

In Portugal, as the trade in spices, silks, and jewels increased, men and women left the countryside, hoping to share in the nation's great new wealth. The more ambitious pursuers of good fortune moved to the east coast of Africa and to India. An estimated 80,000 Portuguese citizens had left their homeland by the time da Gama had become the viceroy of India. But agriculture in Portugal deteriorated as a result. Soon grain and meat were in short supply. People starved and died, while the warehouses of Lisbon overflowed with spices, silks, and ivory.

In the days of Prince Henry and da Gama, Portugal had succeeded despite its small size and population. As other nations discovered new

Portugal extended its influence to include many far-flung places.
This illustration shows a Portuguese fleet off the coast of Brazil,
where the European nation went on to establish
an important base of operations as well.

routes to India, however, the Portuguese were not able to maintain their control in the East. They simply didn't have enough manpower to maintain what they had won with so much bloodshed. In 1570 Muslims attacked *Estado da India*, and in 1585 the Turks drove the Portuguese out of their east African colonies. A century later, Japan banned European trade ships from its harbors. Dutch and British colonies, well funded and well armed, soon outnumbered the Portuguese in Asia.

Afterword

In modern times, it is in Brazil—discovered accidentally by Pedro Cabral in 1500—that Portuguese culture is still most clearly evident. Although Brazil became independent in 1822, Portuguese is the official language, the architecture is distinctly Portuguese, and the country has the largest number of Catholic believers in the world. For good or ill, wherever Portuguese influence can be seen, it is because during the Age of Discovery navigators of that tiny nation, like da Gama, "did not fear their fate too much."

VASCO DA GAMA AND HIS TIMES

1460   Prince Henry dies; Vasco da Gama is born in Sines, Portugal.

1488   Bartolomeu Dias rounds the Cape of Good Hope, the first navigator to do so.

1497   Da Gama leaves Portugal with four vessels to find a sea route to India.

1498   March 2—Da Gama arrives in Mozambique.

        May 20—Da Gama reaches Calicut.

        May 28—Da Gama is escorted to the palace of the *zamorin* where he becomes a virtual prisoner.

        August 29—Da Gama is allowed to set sail for Portugal.

1499   Da Gama's brother Paulo dies at Terceira; several days later, da Gama sails back to Lisbon and is awarded the title of admiral.

1500   Pedro Cabral sets out on a second voyage to India; he accidentally discovers the coast of Brazil.

1502   February 10—Da Gama leads another expedition to India.

        October 1—Da Gama sinks the *Meri*.

1503   February 12—Da Gama attacks a Muslim armada at Calicut.

October 11—Da Gama returns home to Lisbon.

1507   Da Gama is denied control of Sines, his birthplace.

1519   Da Gama becomes count of Vidigueira.

1524   February 24—King John III appoints da Gama viceroy of India.

September—Da Gama arrives in Goa to take up his new post.

December 24—Da Gama dies at Cochin and is laid to rest in a local monastery.

1898   Four hundred years after his first voyage to India, da Gama's remains find a permanent resting place in Restello, Portugal.

Further Research

Books

Aaseng, Nathan. *You Are the Explorer*. Minneapolis: Oliver Press, 1999.

Flowers, Sarah. *The Age of Exploration*. San Diego: Lucent Books, 1999.

Gallagher, Jim. *Vasco da Gama and the Portuguese Explorers*. Philadelphia: Chelsea House Publishers, 2000.

Goodman, Joan Elizabeth. *A Long and Uncertain Journey: The 27,000-Mile Voyage of Vasco da Gama*. New York: Mikaya Press, 2001.

Larkin, Tanya. *Vasco da Gama*. New York: PowerKids Press, 2001.

Stefoff, Rebecca. *Vasco da Gama and the Portuguese Explorers*. New York: Chelsea House Publishers, 1993.

Twist, Clint. *Magellan and Da Gama: To the Far East and Beyond*. Austin, TX: Raintree Steck-Vaughn, 1994.

Web Sites

Admiral Dom Vasco da Gama, Knight Commander of the Military Order of Christ
http://www.angelfire.com/ak/militaryorders/vascogama.html

Chronology of Voyages of Exploration, 1486–1522
http://muweb.millersville.edu/~columbus/data/chr/

Vasco da Gama Seeks Sea Route to India
http://www.oldnewspublishing.com/dagamma.html

"Vasco da Gama" from the *New Catholic Encyclopedia*
http://www.newadvent.org/cathen/06374a.html

Vasco da Gama
http://www.stemnet.nf.ca/cite/exgama.html

BIBLIOGRAPHY

Bell, Christopher Richard. *Portugal and the Quest for the Indies*. New York: Harper & Row, 1974.

Boorstein, Daniel J. *The Discoverers*. New York: Random House, 1983.

Boxer, Charles R. *The Portuguese Seaborne Empire, 1415–1825*. New York: Alfred A. Knopf, 1969.

Cortesão, Armando. *The Mystery of Vasco da Gama*. Coimbra: Agrupamento de Estudos de Cartografia Antiga, Secção Anexa á Universidade de Coimbra; Lisbon: Junta de Investigaçoes do Ultramar, 1973.

Correa, Gaspar. *The Three Voyages of Vasco da Gama*. New York: Burt Franklin, Publisher, 1869.

Divine, David. *The Opening of the World*. New York: G.P. Putnam's Sons, 1973.

Hart, Henry H. *Sea Road to the Indies*. New York: Macmillan Company, 1950.

Kallen, Stuart A. *The 1400s*. San Diego: Greenhaven Press, 2001.

Konstam, Angus. *Historical Atlas of Exploration, 1492–1600*. New York: Checkmark Books, 2000.

Morison, Samuel Eliot. *The Great Explorers: The European Discovery of America*. New York: Oxford University Press, 1978.

Newton, Arthur Perciva. *The Great Age of Discovery*. London: University of London Press, Ltd., 1932.

Prestage, Edgar. *The Portuguese Pioneers*. London: A. & C. Black Ltd., 1933.

Ravenstein, Ernest George. *A Journal of the First Voyage of Vasco da Gama, 1497–1499*. New York: Burt Franklin, Publisher, 1898.

Source Notes

Foreword:

p. 5: "More than any other European nation . . .": Angus Konstam, *Historical Atlas of Exploration, 1492–1600* (Checkmark Books, 2000), p. 14.

p. 6: "warm port": George Sanderlin, *Eastward to India: Vasco da Gama's Voyage* (Harper & Row Publishers, 1965), p. xvi.

p. 6: "did not fear their fate": K. G. Jayne, *Vasco da Gama and His Successors, 1460–1580* (Metheun & Co., Ltd., 1910), p. 2.

p. 6: "do by sea": David Divine, *The Opening of the World: The Great Age of Maritime Exploration* (G.P. Putnam's Sons, 1973), p. 92.

Chapter 1:

p. 8: "long and honorable history": Henry H. Hart, *Sea Road to the Indies* (Macmillan Company, 1950), p. 97.

p. 11: "bold [and] daring": Hart, p. 103.

p. 11: "quick to anger . . . not only for bravery": Hart, p. 103.

p. 11: "One day the king, sitting in his hall . . .": Gaspar Correa, *The Three Voyages of Vasco da Gama* (Burt Franklin, 1869), p. 29.

p. 13: "affairs of the sea . . .": Milton Lomask, *Great Lives* (Charles Scribner's Sons, 1988), p. 113.

p. 13: "Do any and all things necessary": Hart, p. 104.

p. 13: "in the manner in which it had been taken": Hart, p. 104.

p. 13: "My heart tells me": Correa, p. 31.

p. 14: "according to your will and pleasure": Correa, p. 31.

p. 14: "Call him to go with you": Correa, p. 30.

p. 14: "For love of you I pardon him": Hart, p. 107.

p. 15: "to adventure them . . . where, if they survived": Hart, p. 109.

p. 16: "rode the water like ducks": Jayne, p. 35.

p. 16: "on the symbol of this cross": Hart, p. 111.

Source Notes

Chapter 2:

p. 19: "We therefore made sail": E. G. Ravenstein, *A Journal of the First Voyage of Vasco da Gama 1497–1499* (Burt Franklin, 1898), p. 2.

p. 20: "act of superlative audacity": Samuel Eliot Morison, *The Great Explorers: The European Discovery of America* (Oxford University Press, Inc., 1978), p. 105.

p. 22: "No one has yet succeeded": Ravenstein, p. xxvi.

p. 22: "we others . . . humble condition": Ravenstein, p. xxvii.

p. 22: "seemed to sob": Hart, p. 130.

p. 23: "tawny-coloured [and] dressed in skins": Ravenstein, p. 6.

p. 24: "the kindliness of Paulo da Gama": Hart, p. 138.

p. 24: "[Scurvy] rotted my gums": Hart, pp. 136–137.

p. 24: "happened because we looked upon": Ravenstein, p. 8.

p. 26: "we beheld the Cape": Ravenstein, p. 9.

p. 26: "we broke up our store-ship": Ravenstein, p. 10.

p. 26: "We found him very fat": Ravenstein, p. 11.

p. 26: "When about to set sail": Ravenstein, p. 13.

p. 26: "tall people": Ravenstein, p. 17.

p. 28: "just like those of Portugal": Ravenstein, p. 17.

p. 28: "The houses [here] are built of straw . . . long bows and arrows": Ravenstein, pp. 17–18.

p. 30: "gold, silver, cloves": Sarah Flowers, *The Age of Exploration* (Lucent Books, 1999), p. 43.

Chapter 3:

p. 31: "whitewashed stone houses": Hart, p. 149.

p. 31: "for he was already suspicious": Hart, p. 149.

p. 31 : "a sheep, large quantities or oranges": Ravenstein, p. 36.

p. 31: "everything which he required": Hart, p. 149.

p. 33: "to capture us as soon as we entered port": Ravenstein, p. 37.

p. 33: "These and other wicked tricks": Ravenstein, pp. 37–38.

p. 33: "of distinction": Ravenstein, p. 39.

p. 33: "lofty and well-white-washed houses": Ravenstein, p. 46.

p. 34 : "in meeting this challenge": Hart, p. 142.

p. 35: "two strings of coral": Ravenstein, p. 41.

p. 36: "quantities of cloves": Ravenstein, p 41.

p. 36: "not permitted by his master": Ravenstein, p. 42.

p. 36: "he valued this act more highly": Ravenstein, p. 42.

p. 36: "helpless father": Ravenstein, p. 44.

p. 38: "but little clothing": Hart, p. 154.

p. 39: "These people could not live without roses": Hart, p. 161.

p. 40: "We have arrived": Hart, p. 156.

p. 40: "What brought you hither?": Ravenstein, p. 48.

p. 40: "A lucky venture!": Ravenstein, p. 49.

Chapter 4:

p. 41: "we . . . did not feel comfortable": Ravenstein, p. 50.

p. 42: "We put on our best attire": Ravenstein, p. 51.

p. 42: "We did not go within the chapel": Ravenstein, p. 54.

p. 42: "courtyard of great size": Ravenstein, p. 55.

p. 42: "which is chewed by the people": Ravenstein p. 56.

p. 44: "the white goddess": Hart, p. 177.

p. 46: "fallen upon Mozambique": Hart, p. 181.

p. 47: "Much corn, cloth, iron": Ravenstein, p. 63.

p. 48: "he all but learns to speak": Ravenstein, p. 103.

p. 48: "kept in stables like horses": Ravenstein, p. 103.

p. 49: "sell it . . . to the best advantage": Hart, p. 183.

p. 49: "afforded . . . no opportunity for doing so": Ravenstein, p. 65.

p. 49: "bear it, as they cared nothing for that": Hart, p. 183.

Chapter 5:

p. 52: "feeble winds": Ravenstein, p. 79.

p. 54: "eating much fish": Ravenstein, p. 86.

Source Notes

p. 54: "I assure you that is this state of affairs": Ravenstein, p. 87.

p. 54: "Even iron-willed da Gama": Hart, p. 192.

p. 55: "the Lord gave us such a good wind": Ravenstein, p. 92.

p. 56: "like the good Christian he was": Hart, p. 194.

p. 56: "numb with grief": Sanderlin, p. 141.

p. 56: "better than all else in the world": Hart, p. 194.

p. 57: "God gave the Portuguese a small land": Sanderlin, p. 180.

p. 57: "What he had accomplished": Prestage, p. 266.

p. 57: "done such a great thing": Hart, p. 197.

p. 57 : "Console yourself": Correa, p. 269.

p. 57: "it shall be the same": Correa, p. 269.

p. 59: "As soon as the news": Hart, p. 201.

p. 60: "Vasco da Gama, a nobleman of our household": Sanderlin, pp. 142–143.

p. 61: "the privileges, revenues, and taxes": Hart, p. 204.

Chapter 6:

p. 62: "only six princes of the Church": Jayne, p. 68.

p. 62: "Franciscan friars, and merchants": Jayne, p. 62.

p .63: "to follow the will of God": Hart, p. 209.

p. 64: "*Ladrões, ladrões!*": Hart, p. 211.

p. 64: "put . . . its occupants to the sword": Jayne, p. 63.

p. 66: "a long surtout": Hart, p. 222.

p. 67: "the honors, pre-eminences, liberties": Jayne, p. 68.

p. 67: "to ransom every Christian slave": Jayne, p. 65.

p. 67: "the admiral set that ship ablaze": Hart, p. 229.

p. 69: "a contrary wind": Hart, p. 233.

p. 69: "meted out to those who do not obey": Hart, 235.

p. 70: "a broad trail of fire, blood, and hatred": Hart, p. 233.

p. 70 : "the devil entered a Portuguese": Hart, 233.

p. 71: "we command you to remain": Hart, p. 237.

93

p. 71: "irrevocable for all time": Hart, p. 237.

p. 72: "rode to his coronation": Hart, p. 240.

Chapter 7:

p. 75: "on account of the quarrels and plots": Hart, p. 253.

p. 75: "Any woman . . . found in the ships": Hart, p. 253.

p. 76: "Friends, rejoice and be happy": Hart, p. 254.

p. 77: "never shall they meet": Correa, p. 395.

p. 78: "[da Gama] was served by men bearing silver maces": Correa, pp. 380–381.

p. 78: "He was a very disdainful man": Correa, p. 381.

p. 78: "he took much pleasure": Correa, p. 387.

p. 78: "rich gold stuffs, pearls, and jewelry": Hart, p. 256.

p. 80: "great pains in the neck": Correa, p. 426.

p. 81: "It pleased the Lord to give": Correa, p. 427.

p. 81: "Here lies the great argonaut": Hart, p. 260.

p. 82: "Thus we departed": Hart, p. 265.

Afterword:

p. 85: "did not fear their fate too much": Jayne, p. 2.

INDEX

Page numbers in **boldface** are illustrations.